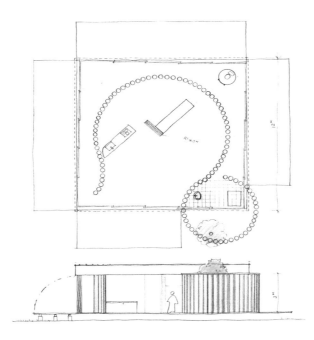

Philip Jodidio

SHIGERU BAN

1957

Architecture of Surprise

TASCHEN

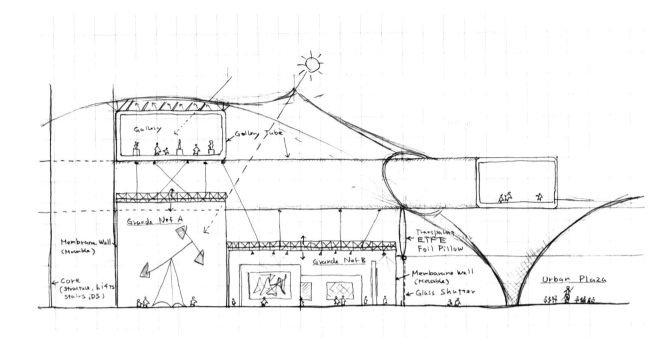

Illustration page 1: Paper House, Lake Yamanaka, Yamanashi, Japan, 1995

Illustration page 2: Shigeru Ban, 2012

Illustration page 4: Centre Pompidou-Metz, France, 2010

© 2012 TASCHEN GmbH
Hohenzollernring 53, D–50672 Köln
www.taschen.com

Editor: Florian Kobler, Cologne
Design: Sense/Net, Andy Disl and
Birgit Eichwede, Cologne
Collaboration: Inga Hallsson, Cologne
Production: Frauke Kaiser, Cologne
Final Artwork: Tanja da Silva, Cologne

ISBN 978–3–8365–3076–7
Printed in Germany

Contents

Architecture of Surprise

Frei Otto and Shigeru Ban, Frei Otto Atelier Warmbronn, 1998.

An architect's office says a good deal about the person. Grand or discreet, these places of work are in themselves a statement and a clue to the personality and the inventiveness of the individual. Shigeru Ban of course has an office in Tokyo, but his Paper Temporary Studio in Paris is a most eloquent evocation of his nature. It was in 2004 that he created this 115-square-meter temporary office (see page 58) on a sixth-floor terrace of the Centre Pompidou in Paris. With its roof made of titanium dioxide PTFE membrane, regular PTFE membrane, and PVC membrane, the tubular form of the office stands out against the metallic substance of the Piano & Rogers building. The interior is finished with tile carpet, wood deck, and Vitra furniture, but Shigeru Ban's own very small office cubicle has a cardboard desk and chairs. It is, of course, significant that he has chosen this apparently most ephemeral of materials to mark his presence during the course of the design and construction of the Centre Pompidou-Metz (Metz, France, 2007–10; see page 80). The modest size of his office and the materials used, typically a derivative of paper, a favored and thoroughly unexpected material of the architect, may recall his Japanese culture, but they also speak of his quiet modesty, a quality not frequent amongst the best-known architects in the world, a select company that he has certainly joined. He is thus in no way typical, neither in his background nor in his choices of places of work and materials. Shigeru Ban states: "The tubular form of the structure is obviously related to the design of the Centre Pompidou itself, but that also happens to be the most efficient shape. In the original design of Piano & Rogers, they proposed to have some temporary structures in or around the building—on the parvis for example. It was necessary to get the permission of Renzo Piano for this design and he accepted it quite happily. He told me also that when he and Rogers won the Centre Pompidou project, they created a temporary office on a boat anchored on the banks of the Seine. In a way, this temporary office is thus connected to the history of the Centre Pompidou. Piano warned me, though, that it is not a good idea to be too close to the client. He was right."

Perched on the Roof
The genesis of this unusual presence of Shigeru Ban and his team on the roof of the Centre Pompidou in Paris is also an interesting clue to his personality and determination. After winning the competition for the Centre Pompidou-Metz extension for the Paris institution, he explains: "I suggested half jokingly to Bruno Racine, the president

Opposite page:
Centre Pompidou-Metz, Metz, France, 2010
In front of the main entrance to the museum.

7

of the Centre Pompidou: 'the agreed design fee is not sufficient for an architectural office from a foreign country like us to rent an office in Paris. So if you could lend us space on the terrace, we can build our temporary office.'" Racine accepted under three conditions: that the terrace could be used free of charge for approximately three years, the expected completion date of the Centre Pompidou-Metz, with other costs to be borne by the architect; that the inside of the office be visible to visitors to the Centre; and that the structure be donated to the Centre Pompidou after its use. "I thought," says Shigeru Ban, "that it is good to be close to the client. Often, when a foreign architect wins a major project in any country, they are supposed to work in conjunction with a large local firm. There have been problems with this kind of collaboration, since the local architect inevitably sides with the client, especially for budgetary matters or for scheduling, instead of supporting the original architect's idea. For them, the client is more important than the foreign architect who happens to be their partner. If design architects visit only once in a while or send their staff, it is very difficult to follow through on a concept to the very end. Clients who do not intervene much in their work spoil Japanese architects. If an architect is famous or has won a competition, the client remains peaceful. We also have very good contractors, so it is easy to build in Japan. Some very famous Japanese architects have discovered after winning a competition that the completed building is entirely different from what they designed. It is because of this problem that I thought it was very important to be near the client." The complex situation surrounding the realization of the Centre Pompidou-Metz led Ban more recently to say that Renzo Piano was right when he had said that it might not have been such a good idea to be so close to the client, but, in the end, the Japanese architect has attained almost everything he wanted, including design control over his most substantial project to date, the new museum building in the east of France.

Paper Temporary Studio, Paris, France, 2004
In its location on top of the Centre Pompidou.

Although Shigeru Ban does not speak specifically of Renzo Piano or Richard Rogers, the fact that his studio is perched on top of their seminal 1977 building says something about the younger architect's attachment to modernity and also to innovation, or, to put it in more traditional terms, an attachment to those who have gone before him. Shigeru Ban builds not only on his own innovations but also on the work of engineers, such as the Japanese structural engineer Gengo Matsui, the American architect John Hejduk, and the German architect Frei Otto, or the engineer Cecil Balmond. Few are likely to be thinking of these figures as being a source of inspiration for a younger Japanese architect, but this is the rather cosmopolitan way that Shigeru Ban has gone about creating his personal pantheon, his starting points in creativity and design, as it were.

Desperately Seeking Hejduk
Born in 1957 in Tokyo, Shigeru Ban studied at the Southern California Institute of Architecture (SCI-Arc) from 1977 to 1980. He attended the Cooper Union School of Architecture, where he studied under John Hejduk (1980–82/83–84). He worked in the office of Arata Isozaki (1982–83), before founding his own firm in Tokyo in 1985. Few noted Japanese architects, with the exception of figures like Fumihiko Maki or Yoshio Taniguchi, have studied outside Japan. In his cosmopolitan education, Shigeru Ban might well be termed the worthy successor of these two elder statesmen of Japanese architecture, and yet his is a route that has differed even more than might be expected from those of Maki or Taniguchi. Shigeru Ban's own explanation of his path from Japan to New York, where he completed his studies, is worth quoting at length, because it

Paper Temporary Studio, Paris, France, 2004
Round openings provided daylight to the architects working in the studio.

reveals his determination and the origin of his unusual work. He traces some of his own drive to childhood experiences. "At first, I wanted to be a carpenter," he says. "My parents extended their house on several occasions, so it seemed that there was always a carpenter working in the house. As a child, I would pick up the small leftover pieces of wood to make something out of them, like a model train or a building. Perhaps it has to do with the education my parents gave me, but I hate to throw things away. I guess, then, that I have a natural predisposition to reuse things." There is also constancy in the motivation of Ban that is admirable in the context of a shifting architectural world today. Again, explaining his early motivations and formative experiences, he says: "To enter the Japanese art school, we had to create a tower higher than one meter just using cardboard, and without wasting materials. Working with strict rules and a limited amount of materials was something I was very good at. I saw my teacher again a few years ago, and he said to me: 'You are still doing the same things.'"

Even today, younger Japanese architects are much more likely to study in their country and to remain in a system that certainly has its virtues, although a real opening to the rest of the world may not be one of them. Shigeru Ban is an exception to almost all the rules that concern the education of Japanese architects, and as his own explanation of his path makes clear, it is his will to follow up on his own sources of admiration or influence that has made him break the molds. "When I was in high school," says the architect, "I was interested in going to art school to study architecture. It was necessary to do a lot of drawings or to make models. One of the best art schools in Japan had a school of architecture and I wanted to go there. I went to a kind of prep school for this type of study and my teacher there was an architect. It was with him in 1975 that I saw a special issue of the magazine *a+u* on John Hejduk. I saw that he taught at Cooper Union in New York. At the time, there was no Internet and nobody really knew much about Cooper Union in Japan. I had to go to the USA and I did not speak any English. I did see in a brochure that they did not accept foreign students unless they transferred from another US institution. I looked for another school of architecture in the US that would admit me so that I could then transfer to Cooper Union. It could have been any school, but, with some luck, I selected SCI-Arc in California. I applied there in 1977 and the school had been established in 1974, so it was a really new school. Eric Owen Moss, Thom Mayne, and Frank Gehry were all involved in it though. They didn't even require an English exam to get in, and because of the portfolio I presented from my Japanese prep school, the Dean of SCi-Arc, Raymond Kappe, admitted me in the second year. SCI-Arc was more interesting than I expected, so I stayed there two and a half years. I still wanted to go to Cooper Union, though, so I was admitted there in the second year, which means I lost the credits I had earned at SCI-Arc. Nonetheless, I managed to do the third and fourth year programs in New York in a single year."

In the Magic Circle
Though he assigns his own good fortune in attending SCI-Arc in its early years to coincidence, it is to be noted that the young man thus found himself in the company of some of the most inventive and significant architects to come forth from the United States in a very long time. Gehry was at the height of his powers in the 1970s, as was the future Pritzker Award winner Thom Mayne of Morphosis. Though his journey to the classroom of John Hejduk appears to have been more willful than accidental, Shigeru Ban has shown a propensity for gravitating toward exceptional, creative figures throughout his career. Without imitating any of them, he appears to have drawn much of his own vital force from their strengths. Then, too, Shigeru Ban has not only sought out figures of note in Japan, like Isozaki or the engineer Gengo Matsui, he has also crossed the path of Americans or Europeans of similar note.

John Hejduk was born in New York in 1929 and died in 1999. He studied at the Cooper Union (1947–50), at the University of Cincinnati (1950–52), and at Harvard (1952–53). He worked in the office of I. M. Pei before setting up his own practice in New York in 1965. He was Dean of Architecture at the Cooper Union beginning in 1975. His career was, in a sense, more devoted to the study and teaching of architecture than to construction, since he built very few permanent structures. He did complete the Kreuzberg Tower and Wings, part of the IBA Social Housing project in Berlin in 1988. Hejduk often designed series of houses, including the so-called Wall Houses (1968–74), of which more than 40 were conceived, but only one (Wall House 2) was built, posthumously, after more than 30 years of hesitation. Hejduk had a considerable influence on the theory and development of architecture in the United States, assuming an almost mythical status during his lifetime. Shigeru Ban makes no secret of Hejduk's influence, particularly on his early career.

Having studied with the American, Ban returned to Japan, perhaps not convinced that he had to follow a different path from that of other architects of his generation, but, nonetheless, embarking on a road that has led him elsewhere. "I don't think I am different," Shigeru Ban says today with certain modesty. He does explain why, in his mind, his creativity took him on a different route. Typically, one discovery led him to another, but Shigeru Ban has maintained a fidelity to his sources and a clarity about them that is atypical in contemporary architecture, where many well-known figures would have the public believe that their work is completely original. "Usually after you graduate from school, you start working for somebody," says Shigeru Ban. "When you start your own practice, you must make some reference to the architect you used to work for. I worked only one year for Arata Isozaki. I admire him greatly, but I don't think I was influenced by his Postmodern style. I particularly liked his Gunma Museum [Mu-

Three Walls House, Setagaya, Tokyo, 1988
In its dense urban setting, the concrete frame of the Three Walls House, with its five openings.

Paper House, Lake Yamanaka, Yamanashi, Japan, 1995
Paper tubes draw a limit between public and private space, interior and exterior.

If not otherwise indicated, all quotes come from the interviews with Shigeru Ban by the author, Paris, July 23 and December 9, 2008.

1 John Hejduk's Wall House was designed in 1973 for Ed Bye, in Ridgefield, Connecticut, USA.

seum of Modern Art, Gunma, Japan, 1971–74] and from the time I was a high-school student I wanted to work for him."

As Shigeru Ban explains, the experience with Isozaki confirmed the influence of his former professor at Cooper Union: "My lack of interest in Isozaki's Postmodernism led me to another influence—that of John Hejduk. Even the titles of my early works, like the Three Walls [Setagaya, Tokyo, Japan, 1987–88] or the Nine-Square Grid House [Hadano, Kanagawa, Japan, 1997], were a kind of homage to him, and to works such as his Wall House."[1] Concluding this explanation of the influence of John Hejduk, Shigeru Ban plays on the appellation most frequently given to architects like the American, who have built very little. Asked if he was disturbed by this lack of actual construction, Ban says: "No, I found his ideas and his vocabulary very realistic on the contrary. And studying with him, it just seemed natural that I had to become a 'paper architect.'" Shigeru Ban has indeed become a "paper architect" but of a different source, one who has actually sought to build with paper.

Functional Duality

The story of how Shigeru Ban first came to use paper in his work is worth telling because it relates a chain of events and influences that have marked his career in more ways than one. With the assistance of Arata Isozaki, Shigeru Ban worked on the exhibition design of three shows at the Axis Gallery in Tokyo. "I worked on an exhibition on Emilio Ambasz [Axis Gallery, 1985]," says Shigeru Ban. "I was interested in Ambasz because he is a graphic and industrial designer, as well as an architect. I was also interested in his way of presenting things—there is always a very functional idea behind his projects. For the Seville 1992 Exhibition, he tried to convince every country to design a pavilion like a ship for the 400th anniversary of the voyage of Christopher Columbus. Since the Expo events are temporary, he imagined ships that could arrive and then leave just as easily as they got to Seville. What remained would have been a pond and park he had designed. The way he presents things to clients, they always have two functions." This functional duality is a clear and present element in the work of Shigeru Ban, where service cores support roofs or floor plates, and the practicality of a shipping container is related not only to its form but to the fact that it is a ubiquitous fixture of the modern world.

Emilio Ambasz was born in 1943 in Argentina, and studied at Princeton University. He served as Curator of Design at the Museum of Modern Art in New York (1970–76), where he directed and installed numerous exhibitions on architecture and industrial design. Ambasz states: "It is my deep belief that design is an act of invention. I believe that its real task begins once functional and behavioral needs have been satisfied. It is not hunger, but love and fear, and sometimes wonder, which make us create. Our milieu may change from generation to generation, but the task, I believe, remains the same: to give poetic form to the pragmatic."[2] Aside from the functional duality he learned from Ambasz, Ban came across a transformative material when he was working on the show devoted to the Argentine-American. "For this first exhibition at the Axis Gallery," he says, "I used some special fabric to make spaces. When we had finished hanging the fabric, only the paper tubes remained. Instead of throwing them away, I brought them back to my office."

From Futagawa to Aalto

As coincidence would have it, Ban's second show at the Axis Gallery was devoted to the Finnish architect Alvar Aalto (Tokyo, Japan, 1986; see page 26). "I was not at all interested in Alvar Aalto when I was a student," explains Shigeru Ban. "My first job when I graduated from Cooper Union was working for the architectural photographer Yukio Futagawa as his assistant. He took me to Finland, and I can say that I was really 'shocked' by the discovery of the work of Aalto. I somehow knew from my studies what to expect to see when I went to visit buildings by Le Corbusier or Mies van der Rohe, but when I saw the work of Alvar Aalto, it was somehow out of my experience. His work can only really be experienced when you visit his buildings. His buildings depend on the context, climate, or the different texture of the materials. Since then, I became a great fan of Alvar Aalto." Shigeru Ban worked on the design of the Aalto show, and sought, as has become his fashion, to resolve certain problems with innovative solutions. Here money was an issue, and wood, a favored material of Aalto, was not suitable as a design element for a temporary show. "They had a limited budget," explains

2 Emilio Ambasz, quoted in "Emilio Ambasz," *Wikipedia*, accessed July 12, 2012, http://de.wikipedia.org:80/wiki/Emilio_Ambasz.

Nomadic Museum, Pier 54, New York, New York, USA, 2005
Designed for "Ashes and Snow," an exhibition of photographs by Gregory Colbert.

Ban, "but I also hated the idea of using a precious material such as wood for a temporary exhibition. I looked for some alternative material to replace wood for the partitions or ceilings and I thought that maybe the paper tubes I had saved from the Ambasz show could be the right solution. So my work in exhibition organization had a very great influence on my career."

The successful installation for the Alvar Aalto exhibition encouraged Shigeru Ban to actually think of using paper tubes as a structural material. "Although I only used it for an interior décor at the time," he says, "I was amazed by the strength and precision and variety of the material. I first proposed a paper structure for an exhibition in Hiroshima that was not realized [Asia Club Pavilion competition, 1989]. The first paper building was a small pavilion for an exhibition in Nagoya [Paper Arbor, Paper Tube Structure 01, Nagoya, 1989]." Today, the use of paper in architecture is seen as a "green" strategy that has brought much attention to Shigeru Ban, but he explains: "Although, now, people think I am an environmentally friendly architect, at that time nobody was talking about the environment. I was interested in raw, cheap materials."

Shigeru Ban has made frequent use of paper tubes in his architecture as the examples published in this book demonstrate. He has also branched out into the use of another unusual construction material, shipping containers. Clearly the idea of saving things that he learned as a child served in the case of the Ambasz and Aalto exhibitions, with the paper tubes saved in the first being used in the second. Might the idea of saving things also have played a role in Ban's use of containers for a traveling exhibition he created a structure for beginning in 2005 (Nomadic Museum, Pier 54, New York, New York, USA, 2004–05; Santa Monica, California, USA, 2005–06; Tokyo, Japan, 2007; see page 62)? "My tendency to save things was not really the issue in this instance," affirms Shigeru Ban. "When I got this commission from the photographer Gregory Colbert, the problem was one of moving a fairly big building from country to country for a traveling exhibition. It had to be easy to build and to dismantle and to be economical to transport. Transporting a building of over 4000 square meters is very expensive. Instead of sending the material, if it is possible to find it on location without shipping, that is the best way to make it economical. Containers are made to an international standard, and we can rent them anywhere in the world. The idea is not so much to reuse materials as it is to use the same material. I had already designed a small exhibition in Tokyo and Osaka using the same idea [Nova Oshima Temporary Showroom, Container Structure, 1996]. These were containers normally meant to store tools and I used them as showcases and also as structures."

Shigeru Ban explains the intellectual influence of Emilio Ambasz when he refers to the dual usage of certain elements of architecture. The Japanese architect, clearly, is also marked by a propensity to save objects like the famous paper tubes. Though he is fascinated by the structural properties of paper when it is thus compressed and formed, his interest appears to be less in the specific material than it is in its properties. This is the link with the shipping containers used for the Nomadic Museum and other projects since that date. The containers are solid, standardized, and yet an unusual element in the composition of architecture, though of course others have employed them to different ends. Most other uses of containers play only on their form, industrial character, or rugged design. Shigeru Ban takes these elements into account but also remembers that containers were made to be moved and are available worldwide. Thus a show held in New York, Santa Monica, and Tokyo would not need to move containers

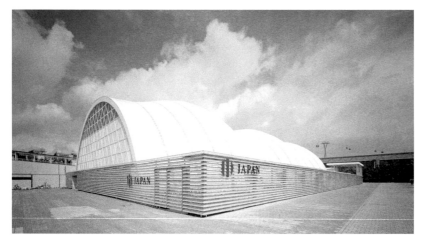

Japan Pavilion Expo 2000, Hanover, Germany, 2000
Designed in collaboration with the German engineer Frei Otto.

since they could be rented in each location. Ban's originality is to seize on this duality or even multiplicity of qualities, while also designing a structure that has a feeling of grandeur, a processional power seen rarely outside religious architecture, and an efficiency in accomplishing its assigned task, that of showing a number of large-format animal photos.

Otto and Matsui

Shigeru Ban's interest in engineering is manifested in many of his buildings, where elements like Vierendeel beams abound. Then, too, making a house without walls requires a solid knowledge of what makes a building stand up. The Japanese architect has extended the interest he expressed early on to meet and work with figures like John Hejduk to the domain of engineering. One such encounter occurred with the German engineer Frei Otto. Frei Otto, winner of the 2005 RIBA Gold Medal, is one of the great figures of 20th-century architecture and engineering. Much of his work has sought to achieve the lightest or most economical solution to a given structural problem, whence his abiding interest in natural forms. He created the Institute for Lightweight Structures at the University of Stuttgart in 1964. Beginning in the late 1960s, he began fusing forms found in nature with modern building techniques and, later, with nascent computer technology. His book *Biology and Building* (1972) examined ways in which the light structure of bird skulls could be applied to architecture; a volume published in 1973 explored the beauty and strength of spiderwebs. Yet even before these books were published, he had completed two remarkable tent-like structures whose similarity to natural forms is clear. His German Pavilion for Montreal's Expo 67 (with architect Rolf Gutbrod) was a 7730-square-meter PVC-coated polyester-fabric structure that took only six weeks to build. "I was a fan of Frei Otto when I was at SCI-Arc," explains Shigeru Ban. "I also dreamed of designing Expo structures. When I got the commission to design the Japanese Pavilion at the Hanover exhibition [Japan Pavilion, Expo 2000, Hanover, Germany, 1999–2000; see page 46], I immediately thought that I needed a local, strong architect or engineer to help me. When I began to design the paper tube structures in 1988, there was a very important Japanese structural engineer, Professor Gengo Matsui. I went to see him and he was interested in supporting me. He was already very famous, so he didn't charge me anything! He was so old that he didn't use

Japan Pavilion Expo 2000, Hanover, Germany, 2000
Construction photos show the complex underlying structure.

a calculator, but a slide rule instead. With this kind of calculation, I could imagine the entire design process. If you use a computer in such cases, the process is inside the black box—you just know the input and the output. My people use computers, but I make sketches." In an event that seems a kind of reward for his continued interest in engineering, in 2001 Shigeru Ban won the prestigious Gengo Matsui Award for the Japan Pavilion. This prize was established in 1991 to commemorate the retirement of the late Gengo Matsui, who was a Professor Emeritus of Waseda University.

As the title of Frei Otto's book *Biology and Building* implies, the German has deviated quite far from what might be imagined as the modern vocabulary, daring to think outside the grid, as it were. This is surely something that he shares with Shigeru Ban, although the Japanese architect appears never to have been quite so literal in his interpretations of any natural phenomena, aside from the physical realities of engineering. As his recent roof for the Centre Pompidou-Metz demonstrates, both the influence of Otto and the thought of natural forms are not far from his mind, even when he is by no means seeking to weave the spider's web that seems to be the model for Otto's roofs of the Munich Olympic Stadium. It is important to understand that Shigeru Ban has long been open to varied influences, actively seeking contact with individuals he finds interesting, learning from them but then totally absorbing part of their thought process into his own method.

Paper Shelter

The career of Shigeru Ban has been marked not only by the use of innovative materials and designs, but also by the application of those elements to types of structures that normally do not attract the active attention of well-known architects. One of these is refugee relief shelters. Though circumstances drew him further into this type of effort than he might have expected, Shigeru Ban, as usual, has a carefully reasoned approach to an aspect of his work that is atypical. In fact, he began to think of this issue at the very outset of his professional career, after his studies in the United States. "When I came back to Japan, I was surprised that architects were not really very respected here," he says. "It occurred to me that this might be due to the history of Japan. Until relatively recent times, there were no architects in Japan—only master craftsmen, like carpenters, who designed and built buildings. At the end of the Meiji Period [1868–1912], we invited foreign architects to build in Japan, so architects have been familiar to the Japanese for only about a hundred years. I thought that maybe this was why they are not so respected."

Commodore Perry and the Taxi Driver

When Commodore Perry viewed the city of Edo, the future Tokyo, during his 1853–54 expedition, he described it as an "extensive plain with a magnificent background of mountains and wooded country." The far-reaching consequences of the Perry Expedition have often been analyzed, but it should be recalled that, as early as 1872, the Meiji government had called on the British architect and planner Thomas Waters to rebuild the sector to the southeast of the Imperial Palace, destroyed in that year by fire. Along a broad avenue, Waters laid out Neoclassical buildings along what became known as the Ginza. Another Englishman, Josiah Conder (1852–1920), built numerous heavy Second Empire-style masonry buildings, such as the National Museum in Ueno Park (1882), which became symbols of the Japanese establishment until the Ministry of

Paper Emergency Shelters UNHCR, Byumba Refugee Camp, Rwanda, 1999
The architect places an emphasis on locally available, inexpensive materials.

the Cabinet decided to call on the Germans Hermann Ende (1829–1907) and Wilhelm Böckmann (1832–1902). Their plan for a Prussian-style building for the Japanese Diet capped with a pagoda-like form met with concerted opposition, and calls for a resolution to the conflict between indigenous and Western architectural styles.[3]

Fully aware of the history of his country, Shigeru Ban did not stop, however, at contemplating the influence of the Perry Expedition and the arrival of foreign architects in Japan. He also sought more contemporary reasons for the lack of respect he perceived for his profession in Japan. "When I take a taxi ride in the countryside in Japan, I sometimes ask the taxi driver who is building this or that building," says Shigeru Ban. "They never mention the name of the architect, only the construction company. They think that the construction company designed the building—this is part of the history of the country. I must admit, too, that although people in many professions make an effort to help society, this is not often the case of architects. Architects often work for privileged clients who want to make their money visible. We help to render their power and money more evident through architecture. When we work for developers, corporations, or governments, it is the same thing. The general public feels that architects make a lot of money working for powerful people. I began to think about what I could do to help society, and, at that time (1994), I was shocked to see photos related to the crisis in Rwanda. I saw, too, that the shelters provided to refugees, even by the United Nations, were of poor quality. I was convinced that we had to improve the shelter, because, otherwise, any medical care would be of no use. I went to the UNHCR Headquarters in Geneva to propose my idea. I was very lucky to be hired as a consultant. Usually the UN provides plastic sheeting and the refugees have to cut trees to make shelters. With a million refugees in Rwanda, the scale of the problem was such that deforestation was a distinct possibility. They tried aluminum pipes, but aluminum is expensive and rare in Africa. The German architect in charge of these programs for UNHCR, Wolfgang Neumann, was looking for other ideas and materials when I arrived. He liked my idea and hired me. The next year, 1995, was the year of the Great Hanshin Earthquake in Kobe. Because I had been working with refugees, I became interested in the plight of

3 William Coaldrake, "Order and Anarchy: Tokyo from 1868 to the Present," in M. Friedman (ed.), *Tokyo, Form and Spirit*, Walker Art Center, Harry N. Abrams, New York, 1986.

Paper Log House, Bhuj, India, 2001
A major earthquake devastated the area in January 2001.

Vietnamese refugees in Kobe after the earthquake. Many of these refugees were living in Kobe and obviously they had a more difficult time than others. They were living just with plastic sheeting and they could not move into the housing proposed by the government outside the city. This was due to the fact that they worked in factories only in a specific area—and could not go so far away. People even tried to kick them out of the park where they were because it was feared that it would become a slum. I thought we had to design some kind of shelter for them. Ideally, such a shelter would be healthier for the people, but also more attractive so that other people in Kobe would accept their presence. After Kobe, I worked in Turkey for disaster relief in 1999, and in India in 2001."

This digression is of interest not only because of the architectural implications of the materials used by Ban, but also because of his careful and thoughtful approach. What led him to disaster relief work was not only an act of pure conscience, but also a response to the question of why architects might not be fully appreciated in Japan. Indeed, Shigeru Ban admits that when these issues arose in his career, he was not as occupied as he is today, but the logic and interest of his application of his talent to these circumstances is significant.

A Bamboo Hat for the Centre Pompidou-Metz
Today, Shigeru Ban spends almost three-quarters of his time outside Japan, and one main reason for this pattern is the fact that he was building the Centre Pompidou-Metz (see page 80), an ambitious extension that the Parisian institution has undertaken in the eastern French city of Metz. The decision to create an extension to the Centre Pompidou was taken in January 2003 by then Minister of Culture, Jean-Jacques Aillagon, and the President of the Centre Pompidou, Bruno Racine. The City of Metz approved the project two months later and an architectural competition was announced on March 18 of the same year. It was imagined by the authorities from the first that the new building should have an architectural impact similar to that created almost 30 years before by Renzo Piano and Richard Rogers in the Beaubourg of Paris. It was also decided that the new building would carry forward the original broad cultural man-

date of the Centre Pompidou, which includes various forms of artistic expression. The program called for just over 12 000 square meters of space, slightly more than a tenth of the size of the Centre Pompidou in Paris. A total of 157 teams from 15 countries submitted for the competition, a group that was reduced on May 27, 2003, to just six projects after six rounds of voting by the jury. The level of the competition was made clear by the list of architects retained for the second phase: Foreign Office Architects (FOA) from London; Herzog & de Meuron from Basel; Stéphane Maupin with the landscape architect Pascal Cribier from Paris; the Rotterdam architect Lars Spuybroek (NOX); Dominique Perrault, the architect of the French National Library, from Paris; and, finally, Shigeru Ban, teamed with Jean de Gastines from Paris and the London architect Philip Gumuchdjian. The project of Shigeru Ban won the jury vote on November 26, 2003, with 14 of the 16 voting members opting for the proposal.

Shigeru Ban explains his participation in the Centre Pompidou-Metz competition in the following terms: "When I heard about the competition, I thought that it would be a very appropriate project for me to participate in. I respect Renzo Piano and Richard Rogers, and I like architecture that is innovative. I saw that the Centre Pompidou was the client and I was sure that they would accept an innovative proposal. I thought that this was a competition that I had to win. I knew that the building was to be in Metz, and I must admit that I did not know much about the city. It was not very important where it was to be since the Centre Pompidou was involved."

Shigeru Ban's design features a surprising woven timber roof, based on a hexagonal pattern, but his proposal to suspend three 90 x 15-meter gallery "tubes" above the required Grand Nef (nave) and Forum spaces was also unexpected and inventive. The nave measures between 8 and 15 meters in height for the exhibition of large works of contemporary art, but the Centre Pompidou-Metz also includes exhibition galleries of different sizes, a creative studio, a conference center and cinema, a documentation

Centre Pompidou-Metz, Metz, France, 2010
Seen here against the background of the rich historic architecture of Metz.

Centre Pompidou-Metz, Metz, France, 2010
The roof design was inspired by a Chinese hat purchased by Shigeru Ban.

and resource center, teaching workshops, a shop, a restaurant and café, administration and management areas, reserves, and technical workshops. Ban explains the remarkable story of the timber roof in an unexpected way: "I happened to buy a Chinese hat in 1998 in Paris. I was working at that time on the Japanese pavilion in Hanover but I was coming almost every weekend to Paris. I saw this hat in a Chinese crafts shop in Saint-Germain-des-Prés and I was astonished at how architectonic it was. The structure is made of bamboo, and there is a layer of oil-paper for waterproofing. There is also a layer of dry leaves for insulation. It is just like architecture for a building. Since I bought this hat, I wanted to design a roof in a similar manner. I designed some daycare centers and I experimented with thin laminated timber roofs using a material similar to what is called glulam[4] in the United States. This story actually goes back to the time I was working with Frei Otto on the Japanese pavilion in Hanover. I saw his Institute for Lightweight Structures [Stuttgart, Germany, 1966–67]. This is a cable structure, but it uses a lot of wood. The cables just form a net and beneath he needed a surface, so he put a lot of timber behind. My thought was that a structure like this could exist just with the timber, without any cables behind. You need a surface, so why not combine its functions to create the structure as well? This realization brought me back to the bamboo hat. I, of course, admire the work of Frei Otto, but I wanted to do something different. We needed a surface, so why have cables as well? I always like to use material as little as possible. My first thought was to have a big roof that would have extended over a garden in Metz."

Images of the Centre Pompidou-Metz give the impression that Ban might well have been inspired by the great spiderwebs of Frei Otto's engineering feat for the Munich Olympic Stadium, and yet his explanation of the origin of the idea takes the viewer on another tangent. There is no desire to be "oriental" in any sense in this roof, rather one to be efficient and innovative. Fundamentally, the roof is also the product of the manipulation of a hexagonal grid through three dimensions, a procedure that even some Modernists might find acceptable. There is a fusion of influences at play in the roof of the Centre Pompidou-Metz and these speak in an eloquent manner of the thought process and method of Shigeru Ban. There is something very new about the design, and yet it blends harmoniously with a rigorous program and a coherent structure. Just as the Centre Pompidou in Paris was an unusual apparition on the international architecture scene, and one that has known continued public success since 1977, so, too, the work of Shigeru Ban in Metz will in all probability mark a shift in architectural sensibility.

An Engineer and a Gardener
Another great engineer, Cecil Balmond from the office of Arup in London, also influenced the concept of the Metz project. Ban explains: "I originally worked with Cecil Balmond on this project in London, but Arup has a team specialized in French projects and I was obliged to work with them once we were selected. They did not agree with my design, so I ended up with something different from my idea and also twice over budget. The client forced us to use steel for the roof instead of wood. I had a gut feeling that I could design the original roof within the allotted budget, but I needed an engineer to prove it. I gave up on Arup and searched in Germany and Switzerland before finding a very good timber specialist in Switzerland, Hermann Blumer, and a timber contractor from Germany. The engineer, without having seen my precise structural

4   Glued laminated timber, also called "gluelam" or "glulam," is a structural timber product composed of several layers of dimensioned lumber glued together.

ideas, brought back the same proposal I had made to the French team of Arup and which they had rejected. My original proposal was the most efficient. Finally, the roof has returned to my original idea—timber is being used as well. The only thing that has changed since the original competition is that I had to reduce the building a bit. I was oversize in my submission. The final concept is thus unchanged."

The Metz building is set in a 2.5-hectare park area and Ban had a plan for that as well. "The site is quite large, and, at the outset, we were supposed to design a park or garden around the building. I worked with Michel Desvigne for the park design but I wanted a continuation of interior spaces under the roof outside. I did not want to make a sculptural building that gives visitors the impression that they are not allowed to come into the museum. Rather than a closed façade, I imagined an open, yet covered space around the building. I felt that the site was appropriate to the organization of different functions under this big roof. After the competition I wanted to work with Michel Desvigne, but the city appointed Nicolas Michelin to design the parvis. We retained the idea of glass shutters that can be opened completely, as is the case in some of my other buildings. The interior and exterior spaces will be completely connected. Security requirements oblige us to have a clear entrance, but the spaces, inside and out, will be totally open visually and physically."

It is clear that with a team that originally included Cecil Balmond and Michel Desvigne, one of the most talented landscape designers of the moment, Shigeru Ban had aimed very high with his original competition entry. Few other architects are prepared to give star billing to their associates in these circumstances, but Shigeru Ban was aware of the professional qualities of Balmond and Desvigne and, much as he had gravitated toward Gengo Matsui, John Hejduk, and Frei Otto, here he had made an intelligent assessment not only of the specific project he was working on, but also of the best available talents. If the evolution of the project did not allow either Balmond or Desvigne to follow through to the end, Shigeru Ban, with his office perched on the Centre Pompidou in Paris, did everything necessary to be able to carry out a scheme as close to the original idea as possible.

Haesley Nine Bridges Golf Club House, Yeoju, Gyeonggi, South Korea, 2010
The treelike timber columns reach a height of three stories.

The Forum and the Grande Nef
Although he had worked on exhibitions and some larger buildings or exhibition spaces like the Nomadic Museum, at Metz, Shigeru Ban enters a different category of architecture and faces the very specific problem of the museum. When asked if he imagined the shell of the building or its interior first, he replied: "The two came together. Many architects make buildings that are difficult to use as museums. Museum people and artists always say that they don't need architects. They prefer industrial spaces such as the ones used at DIA Beacon [OpenOffice, Beacon, New York, USA, 2004], or Tate Modern [Herzog & de Meuron, London, UK, 2000]. They say that architects design museums more for themselves than for the art. I wanted to design something that would be a good museum, but also send a strong message. In the original program, it was requested of the architects that they design gallery spaces in modules 15 meters wide with different lengths. I thought that a useful gallery should have as much wall space as possible, with the best climate control available. I thought of tubes because they have a maximum amount of wall surface—they are in boxes that are very easy to control in terms of climate. Another characteristic of the program is the Grande Nef (nave) space with a very high ceiling. Because the Centre Pompidou in Paris does not

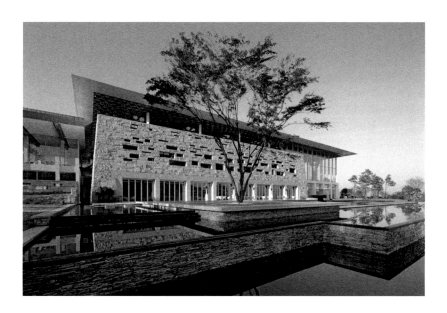

Haesley Nine Bridges Golf Club House, Yeoju, Gyeonggi, South Korea, 2010
Random rubble masonry is used for the base of the structure, with glass curtain walls and timber columns above.

have sufficient high-ceilinged space, there are parts of the collection that cannot be shown to the public, so the Grand Nef is important to the museum. I decided to place the galleries in the form of rectangular tubes, stacked above the Grand Nef. The Forum and Grand Nef spaces are thus created by the hanging tubes and the roof. The roof is not symmetrical like the hat because of the content of the building. If you see the roof from above, however, the basic shape is still a symmetrical hexagon pattern."

Shigeru Ban's decision to set up an office in Paris for the duration of the Metz project is based on his prior analysis of working conditions in such circumstances. In Japan, many of the forces that play on large public projects in Europe do not exist. "That is why I decided to open an office here, in Paris," says Ban. "When some noted Japanese architects were selected to build museums in the United States, they had to change their designs again and again. I discovered that architects are actually very spoiled in Japan. If you are famous, or if you just win a competition, nobody tells you what to do, you can just build, and the contractors support you. It is easy to build the design you want in high quality. Outside, local architects tend to be on the side of the client, instead of siding with the foreign architect. I thought it was very important for me to control design and construction, so I had to live here for the Centre Pompidou-Metz. It is difficult, but I enjoy it. Because I studied in the US perhaps I am more flexible than some other Japanese people."

A House That Is a Window
Although the explanation of the work of an architect usually proceeds from the analysis of specific works, it is clear that the personality and drive of Shigeru Ban have a direct pertinence in helping to understand his buildings. Where it might be assumed today that paper tubes were a carefully thought-out ecological strategy, the reality is that Ban's drive to save and use otherwise discarded materials led him to this innovative solution. Some architects also think of engineers as a necessary evil, but from Gengo Matsui to Cecil Balmond, Shigeru Ban has sought out and found engineers who were interested in collaborating with him in a meaningful way. In the case of Shigeru Ban,

engineering is more than simply assuring that a building will remain standing: it is about seeking innovative solutions to problems that he allows himself to address. Thus, in the case of his Picture Window House (Izu, Shizuoka, Japan, 2001–02; see page 50), a site with a view on Suruga Bay inspired the architect to go far beyond the usual glazed façade that might have been imagined by others. "The first time I set foot on the site, my immediate response was to frame the wonderful view of the ocean stretching horizontally," he says. "That is to say that the building itself should become a picture window. Also, to prevent the architecture from becoming an obstacle disrupting the natural sense of flow from the ocean, I've thought of maintaining that continuity by passing it through the building up to the woods at the top of the hill." The resulting "picture window" is no less than 20 meters long and 2.5 meters high, with an upper story formed by a truss spanning this full length. Invariably, the simple, elegant solutions to relatively complex structural problems are not hidden by Shigeru Ban. The informed eye can follow his reasoning and understand how the spectacular result can seem to be so evident.

Case Study Houses
The chain of reasoning and circumstances that have led Shigeru Ban to many of his ideas have what the French call a *fil rouge*—a recurring drive and insistence on selected goals. Thus, though he modestly says that he wound up at SCI-Arc in the 1970s by a pure coincidence related to his desire to go to Cooper Union, he did find himself there at the heart of a surge of American innovation in architecture unlike any seen since the time of California's own Case Study Houses. A number of Ban's houses carry a primary name, such as the PC Pile House (Susono, Shizuoka, Japan, 1991–92), but also, tellingly, the name Case Study House 02. Shigeru Ban states that his use of this evocative name is the result of two types of observation: "The innovative (experimental) use of new construction methods and, second, the spatial challenge of connecting inside and outside like traditional Japanese houses. I called projects that have these aspects Case Study Houses."[5]

Nine-Square Grid House, Hadano, Kanagawa, Japan, 1997
The house is divided into nine square spaces for a total of 124 square meters.

5   Shigeru Ban, e-mail to the author, December 24, 2008.

PC Pile House, Susono, Shizuoka, Japan, 1992
300-millimeter precast concrete piles support the roof and floor slab.

In 1943, John Entenza, editor of the magazine *Arts & Architecture*, organized a competition under the title "Designs for Post-war Living." Foreseeing a need for large-scale housing construction in the area of Los Angeles, Entenza and Charles Eames wrote an essay in an issue of the magazine published in 1944 calling for the conversion of wartime industrial technologies to the service of home building. The so-called Case Study House program was announced in the January 1945 issue of *Arts & Architecture*. Between that time and 1966, a total of 34 designs, intended as prototypical models of modern architecture for southern California, were published in the magazine, and 23 were actually built. Amongst the eight original participants in the program were Eames, Eero Saarinen, and Richard Neutra. Reflecting the ad hoc nature of the procedure, the houses were numbered in no particular order. One of the most famous of the projects was Case Study House 8 by Charles and Ray Eames, situated in the Pacific Palisades area near a 50-meter-high cliff overlooking the ocean. Completed in 1949, it is considered one of the seminal California modern residential complexes, with home and studio connected by a small garden. The house is known for its use of industrial materials, such as the corrugated metal roof, covered by insulation board. Many of its components were ordered from parts catalogs, and Eames simplified the original plan by redesigning the home after the parts arrived on the site. The reputation of this house was undoubtedly enhanced by the wide distribution of chairs designed by Eames for Herman Miller, such as the famous Eames Lounge Chair (1956).

Located on a two-hectare plot purchased by the magazine, Case Study House 8 is next to House 9, designed by Eames with Eero Saarinen for John Entenza. This residence projects an even more radical simplicity than its neighbor, a theme that recurs in later program houses such as Case Study Houses 21 and 22 by Pierre Koenig. The spare lines and relatively empty interiors of these houses show that a Japanese influence continued to play its role in California architecture, as it had already in Rudolph Schindler's earlier residence (Schindler/Chase House, West Hollywood, USA, 1922). That house mixed a Japanese concept of indoor/outdoor space that is particularly well adapted to the local climate, with a strong rectilinear modernity. It is certainly interesting to note that much of Ban's work adheres precisely to those two criteria, sometimes limited by somewhat cooler climates, as in Metz.

In a way, the voyage of Shigeru Ban to California was a kind of return to the roots of contemporary architecture, not necessarily the more clinical style that evolved from the Bauhaus, but the one that found its points of origin in the architecture of Japan. It was, indeed, here that Rudolph Schindler and others first put into built form ideas that were fundamentally related to the history of Japanese architecture. On November 4, 1935, the German architect Bruno Taut (1880–1938) wrote in his journal: "I can truly claim to be the discoverer of Katsura." This affirmation, concerning the 17th-century imperial residence located near Kyoto, is of considerable importance for the evolution of contemporary Japanese architecture. Whereas the Japanese had in various ways absorbed the Western influences to which they were subjected after the Perry Expedition, they had come to reject many aspects of their own tradition. Thus the rise of fascism in Japan was accompanied by a certain rejection of Western-inspired modernity in favor of an architecture called *teikan yoshiki*, or the "Imperial roof style," which featured heavy cubic structures capped by equally ungainly "Japanese" roofs. Having arrived in Japan in May 1933, Taut spent three and a half years writing about Katsura, linking its elegant simplicity to the goals of the Modern Movement and calling it an

Picture Window House, Izu, Shizuoka, Japan, 2002
The upper story of this house is formed by a truss spanning 20 meters.

"eternal monument." As Arata Isozaki points out, other Western architects, such as the German Gustav Prattz, had visited Katsura even before Taut, and had integrated its lessons into "the renewal of world architecture."[6] The rediscovery of the fundamental links between the purity of Japanese tradition and Modernism itself occurred only after the trauma of World War II, partially because the very idea of calling on tradition had been misappropriated by a largely discredited political ideology.

Ambiguity and Determination
Naming his works after the Case Study Houses is certainly not an innocent gesture on the part of Shigeru Ban. His own work is decidedly modern, as he underlines when pointing out that his admiration of Arata Isozaki stopped short of accepting the elder architect's Postmodern phase. Ban always eschewed using a rigorous Modernist grid in his work, although some of his projects, such as the Nine-Square Grid House (Case Study House 09, Hadano, Kanagawa, Japan, 1997), emphasize the kind of geometric rigor that characterized many of the residences sponsored by *Arts & Architecture*. Where Charles and Ray Eames realized their house with off-the-shelf materials and an intentional visibility of structural elements, Ban, too, has explored industrial elements and has always rendered structure comprehensible in his work. It should be clear, though, that Shigeru Ban has always picked his sources of inspiration with great care. When thinking of the New York Five, he might well have decided that the rigorous white grids of Richard Meier were to his taste, but, instead, he sought out John Hejduk, the paper architect who imagined that a wall could also be a house. Hejduk's curving forms in that instance are also based on rigor in design, but they dance and surprise more than would a white cube. Ban's architecture is, indeed, one of continual surprise and change, despite his tendency to number works as belonging to a series.

Shigeru Ban's work is one of refinement and research, one that builds on what has come before. He looks also to the tradition of his own country, where the ambiguity between exterior and interior is a frequent theme. Then, too, paper is an element of Japanese architecture, albeit used in a fundamentally different way than the structural

6 Arata Isozaki, "Katsura: A Model for Post-Modern Architecture," in *Katsura Villa – Space and Form*, Iwanami Shoten Publishers, Tokyo, 1983.

Villa Vista, Weligama, Sri Lanka, 2010
This house is located on a hilltop site facing the ocean.

paper tube system imagined by Ban. In traditional Japanese architecture, a *shoji* is a door, window, or room divider consisting of translucent paper over a frame of wood or bamboo. Ban's strength lies in being able to interpret ideas or to seek the essence of his own cultural tradition or that which has evolved around modern architecture, for example. Ban is almost never Modernist in the usual sense, preferring to use structural surprises and technical clarity where Modernism often contented itself with rectilinear repetition. In many ways, the Centre Pompidou-Metz, which opened in 2010, is Shigeru Ban's first large-scale work on the international stage. Though other projects like the Nomadic Museum were seen by thousands in New York or Tokyo, the Centre Pompidou-Metz will remain, and its resolution of spatial issues, its design, and its efficiency will all be duly noted in journals of architecture and museum design. The care and effort that Shigeru Ban has put into Metz, even daring to come and sit on the roof of the Centre Pompidou in Paris until the new building was a reality, makes it clear that he understood what is at stake. This project will surely lead to others, and, at the age of 55, Shigeru Ban is just entering into the period when architects of note begin to take their place in international circles. As the contents of this book demonstrate, he has already left his mark where houses, or more unusual forms of construction, such as refugee housing or temporary structures, are concerned. Everything in his method and his character, which is methodical and determined, but often unorthodox, suggests that Shigeru Ban is, indeed, one of the great world figures of his generation in architecture. Circumstances and his own efforts will undoubtedly verify this statement in the years to come.

1986 ▸ Alvar Aalto Exhibition

Axis Gallery, Tokyo, Japan

Shigeru Ban conceived this 1986 installation in Tokyo for an exhibition originally held at New York's Museum of Modern Art ("Alvar Aalto: Furniture and Glass," September 26–November 27, 1984). His intention was to "design the exhibition space as an Aalto-like interior," but a limited budget and the temporary nature of the installation dictated that wood, Aalto's material of predilection, could not be used. These constraints proved to be significant for Shigeru Ban since he determined that tubes made of recycled paper could be used to create the ceilings, partitions, and display stands for the show. As well as evoking the undulating lines of Aalto's wood, this use of paper was ecologically sound, at a time when "green" architecture was not nearly as fashionable as it has become since then. As he says quite simply: "This was the beginning of paper architecture." Shigeru Ban also participated in a more recent Aalto exhibition, at London's Barbican Art Gallery ("Alvar Aalto Through the Eyes of Shigeru Ban," February 22–May 13, 2007), evidence of an ongoing interest on the part of the Japanese architect in his Finnish predecessor. As Ban says: "I admire the works of Alvar Aalto, whose architecture was modern yet regional, and made much use of natural materials and organic curves."

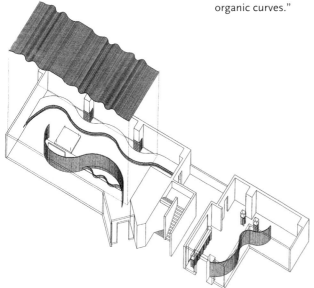

1987 ▸ Villa K

Chino, Nagano, Japan

Above:
The long linear wall defines circulation routes.

Opposite page:
The entry bridge arrives at the second level.

Below:
An elevation drawing showing the tilted roof.

This wooden three-story structure has a total floor area of 115 square meters and is built on a 1220-square-meter site. Designed between October 1986 and February 1987, it was built between April 1987 and August of the same year. Located in a mountainous area of Japan, the residence is entered at the second-floor level via a bridge in order to allow visitors a view of the mountains, blocked on the lower level by dense vegetation. The structure has a sloped roof that forms an equilateral triangle, but more unusual is the idea that the house is really composed of three walls, a curved wall forming a partial circle that "defines the interior space, to which the second linear wall defining circulation routes (stairs and the entrance bridge) is added." A cylindrical core containing kitchen, bathroom spaces, and services forms the third wall and is defined by the architect as the "core of the whole operation of the design." The basic design thus adapts the form of a partially opened fan, radiating from the cylindrical core. Glazed openings between the walls and the roof allow natural light to enter the space and make its structure clear. A large window in the living room frames a view of the mountains in this house that was designed on "the smallest practical module" of 1.5 meters.

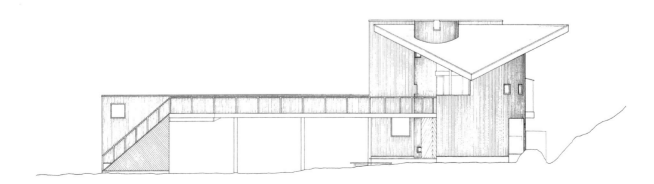

1995 ‣ Furniture House

Lake Yamanaka, Yamanashi, Japan

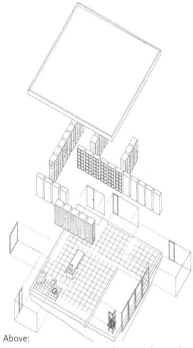

Above:
An exploded axonometric drawing shows the furniture walls.

Opposite page:
The extreme simplicity of the design is visible in the views of the house from the exterior and interior.

Below:
Construction photos show the furniture elements.

Like his earlier House with a Double Roof (Lake Yamanaka, Yamanashi, Japan, 1992–93), Case Study House 04 is also on Lake Yamanaka near Mount Fuji. The 562-square-meter site was used to build a one-story house occupying 111 square meters. The most unusual aspect of this otherwise rather simple design is the use of factory-produced, full-height furniture units that serve as structural elements. Designed between June 1992 and September 1993, the house was built between December 1993 and April 1995. Formed into 80-kilogram units that greatly reduced on-site work and material waste, the 2.4-meter-high furniture units are used as bookshelves and other purposes. The Furniture House was completed three months after the so-called Great Hanshin Earthquake (January 17, 1995), whose epicenter was near Kobe, and Shigeru Ban wrote: "I learned that during the earthquake, many people were hurt by falling furniture or had roofs fall in on them because they were trapped in the spaces between furniture. Furniture is strong and can protect people, so I utilized it as a structural element in the 'furniture apartment' system." The "furniture apartment" system was developed for emergency relief by Ban along lines imagined for the Furniture House.

1995 ‣ Paper House

Lake Yamanaka, Yamanashi, Japan

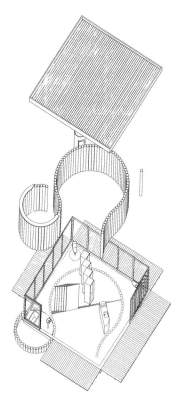

This house, also called Paper Tube Structure 05, was designed on a 499-square-meter site by the architect for his own use. The one-story paper tube structure occupies a total of 100 square meters and has a square plan. It was designed between October 1990 and July 1994, and built between October 1994 and July 1995. A total of 110 paper tubes 2.7 meters high are arranged in an S-shape that defines the spaces of the house. Ban points out that "this project was the first in which paper tubes were authorized to be utilized as a structural material in a permanent building." Given the strict building codes in Japan, this is no small accomplishment. The vertical loads on the house are borne by 10 paper tubes, while the 80 interior tubes carry the lateral stress on the structure. The tubes form an interior living space with a gallery area containing a 123-centimeter paper tube column for the toilet. On the whole, this house expresses an emptiness that is quite frequent in Japanese houses, but which may be somewhat surprising to Westerners. "The living area in the large circle is represented as a universal space with no furnishings other than an isolated kitchen counter, sliding doors, and movable closets," says Ban. Outdoor terraces extend beyond the perimeter of the house, which takes on a classic purity underlined by the repetitive nature of the paper tube columns.

Above:
An exploded axonometric reveals the simple design.

Opposite page:
Curving paper tube walls open to the forest setting.

Right:
Paper tube walls enclose the private space of the house.

1995 ▸ Curtain Wall House

Itabashi, Tokyo, Japan

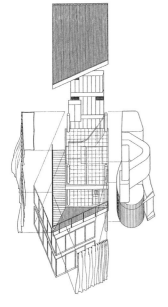

Above:
An exploded axonometric of the house.

Opposite page:
Large-scale curtains replace outer walls.

Also named Case Study House 07, this project is one of the iconic works of Shigeru Ban, challenging as fundamental an idea as the walls of a house with a pertinent analysis and a real design logic. Designed in a one-year period beginning in September 1993, it was built between November 1994 and July 1995. It is a three-story, steel-frame structure with a total floor area of 179 square meters intended as a studio and residence for a client who has what the architect calls an "open and free downtown culture." Playing on the Modernist term "curtain wall," the architect has hung actual tent-like curtains on the façades between the second and third floors on the east and south sides of the building. These curtains cover generous terraces that can be fully exposed when the curtains are opened. External glazed doors and these curtains control light in the house and insulate the residence in winter. Making direct reference to Japanese tradition, Shigeru Ban states: "This thin membrane takes the place of *shoji* screens, *fusuma* doors, shutters, and *sudare* screens in the traditional Japanese house." The basic structure is made of thin columns and slabs, with the "curtain walls" providing the most surprising element of what is otherwise a very light, white construction.

Above:
The house with its "curtain walls" closed.

Right:
A night view with the curtains fully open.

1995/1998/2001 ▸ Paper Log House

Nagata, Kobe, Japan; Kaynaşlı, Turkey; Bhuj, India

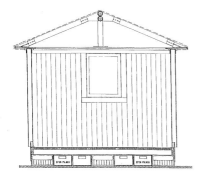

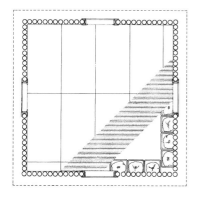

Above:
A basic drawing of the structure.

Opposite page:
The Indian version of the Paper Log House (above) and the Japanese one (below).

Right:
Interior of the Turkish Paper Log House.

Called Paper Tube Structure 07, this one-story temporary residence has a total floor area of 16 square meters. Designed in May and June of 1995, the year of the Great Hanshin Earthquake in Kobe, this house was inspired by the plight of a group of Vietnamese churchgoers who were still living in plastic-sheet tents months after the January 1995 earthquake. Shigeru Ban asked them why and they explained that government-provided housing was located too far away for easy transport and school registration for their children. He decided to create temporary houses for them. Shigeru Ban explains: "The design criteria called for a cheap structure that could be built by anyone, with reasonable insulated properties that was acceptably attractive in appearance. The solution was a foundation of sand-filled beer cases, walls of paper tubes (diameter 108 millimeters, 4 millimeters thick), and with the ceiling and roof made of membrane material. The design was a kind of log-house cabin. The beer cases were rented from the manufacturer and were also used to form steps during the construction process." The simplicity of this process and the fact that the paper tubes could be made on site met all of the criteria for solving difficult living conditions engendered by the earthquake. By the end of the summer of 1995, 27 of these houses had been built for both Vietnamese and Japanese users.

1995/1999 ▸ Paper Church

Nagata, Kobe, Japan; Taomi, Nantou, Taiwan

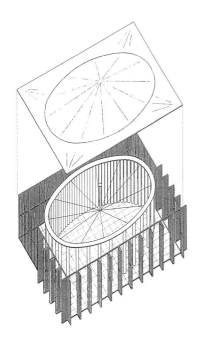

Paper Tube Structure 08 was designed between March and July 1995 and built by 160 volunteer students between July and September of the same year. It was a single-story, 168-square-meter building. This community hall and church was designed to replace the Takatori Church destroyed on the same site by the January 1995 earthquake. Corrugated polycarbonate sheeting was used as a skin and 58 tubes placed in an elliptical pattern, inspired by the church designs of Bernini, formed the structure. Operable glazed screens on the façade between the paper tubes allowed the creation of a continuous space between exterior and interior. The roof was made of tent material, allowing for some penetration of light during the day and a certain glow from the inside at night. The requirement that the church be easily assembled by non-skilled volunteers made Ban imagine that the structure could well be taken apart and used at another disaster site as required. Though made of apparently ephemeral materials, the church celebrated its tenth anniversary in 2005. Disassembled in June 2005, the church was rebuilt in Taiwan in 2008 with the same materials. It was replaced by a new Takatori Church (2006–07; see page 66), also by Shigeru Ban.

Above:
The exploded axonometric drawing shows the plan as an oval inserted in a rectangle.

Opposite page:
The paper tube columns enclose the worship space while also opening to the exterior.

Right:
A façade view of the completed structure.

1997 ▸ Wall-Less House

Karuizawa, Nagano, Japan

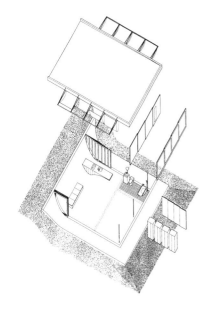

Case Study House 08 was designed between August 1995 and September 1996. It is a one-story, 60-square-meter residence built with a steel frame on a sloping site. Excavated at the rear, the house has a floor that curls up to join the roof at the back, absorbing the horizontal loads. Three very thin columns (55 millimeters in diameter) mark the structure, a solution allowed by the fact that the columns have only vertical loads to bear. Shigeru Ban explains: "In order to express the structural concept as purely as possible all the walls and mullions have been purged leaving only sliding panels. Spatially, the house consists of a 'universal floor' on which the kitchen, bathroom, and toilet are all placed without enclosure, but which can be flexibly partitioned by the sliding doors." Set on a 330-square-meter site, the house reduces the expression of architecture almost to its utmost minimum, and yet this design cannot be called "minimalist" in the traditional sense of clean, white surfaces. With its interior bared and its structural elements almost absent, the Wall-Less House further explores Ban's fascination with challenging the most basic assumptions about architecture.

Above:
Extreme simplicity of design is revealed by this drawing.

Opposite page:
The roof slab is most evident in this photo taken from below.

Right:
The house appears to have only a floor and a ceiling.

1995–99 ▸ Paper Emergency Shelters for the UNHCR

Byumba Refugee Camp, Rwanda

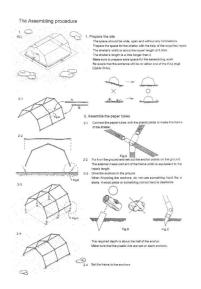

The Assembling procedure

1. Prepare the site
   The space should be wide, open and without any inclinations.
   Prepare the space for the shelter with the help of the supplied ropes.
   The shelter's width is about the ropes' length of 3.50m.
   The shelter's length is a little longer than it.
   Make sure to prepare extra space for the assembling work.
   Be aware that the entrance will be on either one of the End Wall (Gable Side).

2. Assemble the paper tubes
   2-1 Connect the paper tubes with the plastic joints to make the frame of the shelter.
   2-2 Put it on the ground and set out the anchor points on the ground.
   The external measurement of the frame width is equivalent to the rope's length.
   2-3 Drive the anchors in the ground
   When Knocking the anchors, do not use something hard like a stone. A wood piece or something not too hard is desirable.
   The required depth is about the half of the anchor.
   Make sure that the plastic lids are set on each anchors.
   2-4 Set the frame to the anchors.

Fifty examples of Paper Tube Structure 10 were built in Rwanda between February and September 1999. Measuring 1.7 meters high, 3.5 meters wide, and 4 meters long, these shelters were intended to improve on the plastic sheets and hatchets initially provided by the United Nations High Commission for Refugees (UNHCR). Concerns about local deforestation led to the acceptance of Shigeru Ban's proposal to use paper tubes, which were both readily usable and unlikely to be resold or stolen. The first two phases of the project consisted in designing three prototype shelters that were examined for their durability, cost, and resistance to termites. The use of simple machinery for on-site production was analyzed in collaboration with a number of medical relief organizations. Though the crisis in Rwanda generated as many as two million refugees, this effort to find better ways to house people in such catastrophic circumstances could well be seen as the impetus for an improvement of the methods employed by the UNHCR or the various NGOs that assist in these cases. The idea that an inventive architect of Ban's stature might participate in such an effort is certainly new.

Above:
Drawings show how to assemble the shelters.

Opposite page:
The shelters inhabited by Rwandan refugees.

Right:
Assembling the simple paper tube structure.

2000 ▸ Japan Pavilion

Expo 2000, Hanover, Germany

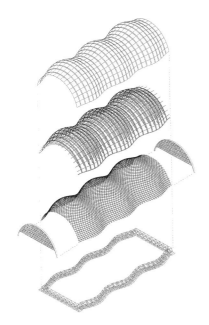

With a total floor area of 3015 square meters and a height of 16 meters, this was the largest of Shigeru Ban's paper tube structures (number 13). The choice of this material was particularly apt for Expo 2000 in Hanover because the exhibition was dedicated to environmental themes, and, in this specific instance, had somehow to reflect Japanese tradition. The use of paper, of course, facilitated the inevitable demolition and recycling of construction materials. The pavilion was designed between July 1997 and August 1999. It is not surprising that Ban called on the celebrated German engineer Frei Otto, as well as the UK engineers Buro Happold, to work with him as he developed the wave-like form made of 440 cardboard rolls measuring 12 centimeters in diameter and up to 40 meters in length. Sonoco Europe, the largest paper tube manufacturer in the region, worked on the development of the construction materials. A paper membrane developed in Japan and made of five fireproof, water-resistant layers was used for the roof covering. Shigeru Ban concludes: "Supported by its many collaborators, the 'Paper Pavilion' is the successful result of multinational collaboration, as well as of the combination of ideas and technologies."

Above:
The undulating or wave-like form of the pavilion seen in an exploded axonometric.

Opposite page:
The membrane covering allows natural light into the building.

Right:
A night view shows the pavilion glowing from within.

2000 ▸ Naked House

Kawagoe, Saitama, Japan

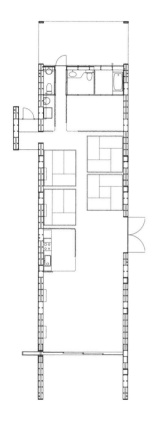

Shigeru Ban has attempted on numerous occasions to redefine the limits of architecture, in particular in his Case Study Houses. In the Naked House (Case Study House 10), located in an agricultural district about 20 kilometers north of Tokyo, he has created a shedlike design with moveable bedroom units that can be rolled into any location, even outside the limits of the house itself. Having been inspired by local materials and agricultural architecture, he employed white extruded polyethylene, a packing material for fruit, in the skin of the shed, which resembles a greenhouse to some extent. Thirty-four arched trusses form the essential shape of the building. Inside, the actual "bedrooms" are made of brown paper-honeycomb panels set on wooden frames, the whole on wheels, each unit measuring a modest six square meters. Bathroom, kitchen, and laundry areas are in fixed locations separated from the rest of the house by high white curtains. The house has a total floor area of 139 square meters and was designed between May 1999 and April 2000, being built between May and November of 2000. Shigeru Ban explains that what the client wanted was a house that "provides the least privacy so that the family members are not secluded from one another; a house that gives everyone the freedom to have individual activities in a shared atmosphere, in the middle of a unified family." He concludes: "This house is, indeed, a result of my vision of enjoyable and flexible living, which evolved from the client's own vision toward a living and a family life."

Above:
The basic rectangular plan can be altered by moving the fixed and moveable units.

Opposite page:
The interior of the house is light and airy, and can be altered by the client.

Right:
The translucent façade of the building at nightfall.

2002 ▸ Picture Window House

Izu, Shizuoka, Japan

Designed between December 1999 and February 2001, this is a 274-square-meter residence. It revolves in good part around a very large 20 x 2.5-meter picture window, with an upper story formed by a truss spanning 20 meters. The site is a hill above Suruga Bay in eastern Japan, and the house is a two-story, steel-frame structure. Shigeru Ban explains: "The first time I set foot on the site, my immediate response was to frame the wonderful view of the ocean stretching horizontally. That is to say that the building itself should become a picture window. Also, to prevent the architecture from becoming an obstacle disrupting the natural sense of flow from the ocean, I've thought of maintaining that continuity by passing it through the building up to the woods at the top of the hill." The single dramatic architectural and engineering gesture chosen by Shigeru Ban to incarnate this house is, indeed, closely related to its site, but also to his own tendency to make each of his buildings assume what might be called a modestly spectacular solution to a given problem.

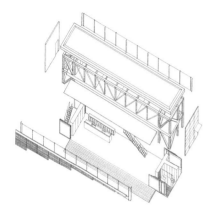

Above:
A drawing shows the basic structural elements.

Opposite page:
The house takes the form of a truss-supported rectangular volume over a large void.

Right:
The column-less ground-floor space offers spectacular views.

2002 ‣ Atsushi Imai Memorial Gymnasium

Odate, Akita, Japan

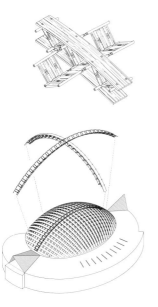

This timber building, also called Plywood Structure 04, is a sports facility designed between February 2000 and August 2001. Located in the far north of the Island of Honshu (like the Imai Hospital Daycare Center, 2000–01), this one-story, timber and reinforced-concrete structure is in the same town as Toyo Ito's Odate Jukai Dome Park (1995–97). The total floor area of the building is 981 square meters, and the site measures 2042 square meters. Intended as a gymnasium and swimming pool, the building uses a laminated veneer lumber (LVL) structural system. Creating a 20 x 28-meter oval dome with the capacity to resist heavy snow loads in the winter was a challenge for Shigeru Ban. He chose to create an LVL space frame with successive wooden arches, proving that thin plywood can be used more effectively on larger spans than might be expected. In much the same way, Shigeru Ban has shown that paper tubes can be employed as structural elements. An added advantage of the system is that it uses much less wood than other systems of lamination. Shigeru Ban does not shy away from questioning some of the most firmly rooted beliefs of the architectural profession, in particular its reliance on tried and true, but often expensive, construction methods. In this he is almost unique, going far beyond the traditional issues of design, dealing, too, with fundamental questions of the use of space. He succeeds in mastering form even as he innovates in other areas.

Above:
Drawings show the laminated veneer lumber system that supports the dome.

Opposite page:
The interior is both simple and elegant, admitting natural light.

Right:
From the exterior the building appears to be a closed shell.

2003 ‣ Glass Shutter House

Meguro, Tokyo, Japan

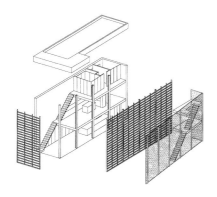

Above:
An exploded drawing shows the house and neighboring grid wall.

Opposite page:
The house's glass shutters entirely open.

Below:
The shutters in their closed position.

Located in the Meguro area of Tokyo, this combined residence and restaurant was designed between June and November 2001 and is set on a small 133-square-meter site. It was built for a chef well known for his television appearances and his cooking school, also located in the new structure. The building area is just 74 square meters and the total floor area is 152 square meters. The three-story, 4 x 16-meter, steel-frame house is remarkable because two of its façades open entirely from street level to roof. Rolling glass shutters disappear into the roof, allowing an outside patio with a bamboo wall to become an integral part of the restaurant in warm weather. Local regulations would normally permit only two stories on this site, but, as Shigeru Ban says: "The three-story volume which has only two floors is legally considered to be two-storied. The stairs connecting to the second level legally mean a floor dividing the first and the second floor. The whole volume is equivalent to three ordinary stories. The completed building has a restaurant on the ground floor, a kitchen-studio on the second, and housing on the third floor. Each area vertically conveys a sense of unity and the border-line—workplace or housing—is intentionally unclear." Ban concludes: "I have tried to connect inner space to the outside by using consecutive outward-opening doors in a series of housing projects. The shutters can be fully opened or be set at the height of each floor, which enables inner space to connect to outside in various ways and to be barrier free. Also, the fence made of bamboo defines the border to the neighboring site and secures its privacy." Because of its refined support design, the Glass Shutter House is extremely light and airy, giving new meaning to the typical Japanese idea of "in-between space."

2003 ‣ Shutter House for a Photographer

Minato, Tokyo, Japan

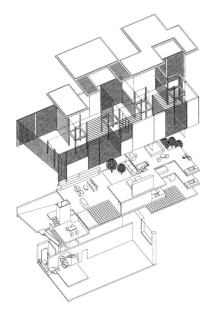

Designed for a successful photographer, this house is unusual in that it stands on a long, rectangular plot of land in the heart of Tokyo, and has a considerable floor area by Japanese standards (465 square meters, comprising a basement and three stories above grade). The actual building, designed between February 2000 and August 2002, covers only 142 square meters, however. Made of concrete, steel-reinforced-concrete, and steel, it is part of a series of buildings designed by Shigeru Ban with rolling shutters that can be opened completely when weather allows. Ultimately, these shutters can serve to dissolve the boundaries between interior and exterior. The photographer told the architect: "If only Mies had been alive, I would have commissioned him..." Ban's response was to create strict grid modules, four meters and two meters on a side, that make up all the rooms and the interior courtyards. A canopy of thin louvers and full-height glazing facing the inner courtyards gives ample natural light to the house. A high, checkerboard screen with ivy growing from it surrounds the house on all sides to give sufficient privacy. A large, underground studio protected from the light was designed for the photographer. With typical humor, Ban says: "I was relieved, after completion, to hear the client say, in a casual manner, 'it was better than asking Mies to do it.'"

Above:
A drawing reveals the complexity and size of the structure.

Opposite page:
Ground-floor interior spaces open into the courtyards.

Right:
The house seen from its Tokyo residential street.

2004 ▸ Paper Temporary Studio

Centre Pompidou, Paris, France

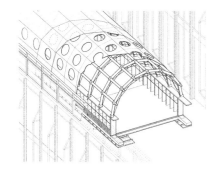

Having been selected to design the Centre Pompidou-Metz (Metz, France, 2007–10; see page 80), Shigeru Ban jokingly suggested to the president of the Centre Pompidou in Paris that he would not be able to carry out the project for the agreed design fee unless he could place a temporary studio on a terrace of the celebrated Piano & Rogers building. In 2004, Ban created this 115-square-meter temporary office, a paper tube structure with some timber joints and steel cables. The roof is made of a titanium dioxide PTFE membrane, a regular PTFE membrane, and a PVC membrane. The interior is finished with tile carpet, wood deck, and Vitra furniture. Local architecture students carried out construction with Ban's Japanese students. Shigeru Ban says: "The tubular form of the structure is obviously related to the design of the Centre Pompidou itself, but that also happens to be the most efficient shape. In the original design of Piano & Rogers, they proposed to have some temporary structures in or around the building—on the parvis for example. It was necessary to get the permission of Renzo Piano for this design and he accepted it quite happily." Despite its restrained size, the location of this studio on the top floor of the Centre Pompidou, near the Georges Restaurant and above all the temporary exhibition galleries of the Centre, assures that it may well be Shigeru Ban's most frequently viewed work.

Above, top:
A drawing showing the layers that make up the structure.

Above, bottom:
An interior view of the studio whose work was intended to be visible to museum visitors.

Opposite page:
The studio in its rooftop setting on the Piano & Rogers building.

2006 ▸ Seikei University Library

Musashino, Tokyo, Japan

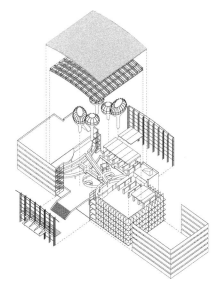

This library, large by the usual standards of Shigeru Ban's buildings, has a floor area of 11996 square meters and was designed between September 2003 and December 2004. It is a steel-frame, precast-concrete, steel-reinforced-concrete, and wood structure. The architect states: "A traditional library is defined as a quiet place for study, yet the new Seikei University Library defines a new idea that embraces all forms of communication and information exchange. The large, glazed, transparent atrium located in the center of the building accommodates several freestanding pods for gathering and information exchange." These pods, attached by platforms and bridges, mark the interior of the structure, creating an animated atmosphere that the large, gently curved exterior roof does not lead the visitor to expect.

Above:
An exploded axonometric drawing shows the entire structure.

Opposite page:
The freestanding pods that stand in the atrium.

Right:
The main façade of the library showing the central atrium.

2005/06/07 ▸ Nomadic Museum

Pier 54, New York, New York, USA;
Santa Monica, California, USA; Tokyo, Japan

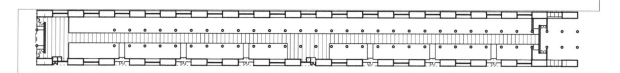

The Nomadic Museum was a 4180-square-meter structure intended to house "Ashes and Snow," an exhibition of large-scale photographs by Gregory Colbert, on view in New York from March 5 to June 6, 2005. It was re-created subsequently in Santa Monica, California, and in Tokyo. No less than 205 meters long, the 16-meter-high, rectangular building was made up essentially of steel shipping containers and paper tubes made from recycled paper, with inner and outer waterproof membranes and coated with a waterproof sealant. Located on Pier 54 on Manhattan's Lower West Side, the building had a central 3.6-meter-wide wooden walkway, composed of recycled scaffolding planks, lined on either side with river stones. The overall impression of this structure was not unlike that of a temple, or, as the architect wrote: "The simple, triangular, gable design of the roof structure and ceremonial, columnar interior walkway of the museum echo the atmosphere of a classical church." The first building to be made from shipping containers in New York, the Nomadic Museum is an intriguing effort to employ recyclable materials to create a large-scale structure. Despite the rather difficult access to the site and high entrance fee, many New Yorkers went to visit Ban's museum, perhaps more intrigued by its spectacular outer and interior forms than by the theatrical photographs of Colbert.

Above:
A floor plan of the long, rectangular structure.

Opposite page:
The Nomadic Museum in its New York setting.

Right:
Large paper tubes support the roof of the structure.

2006 › Papertainer Museum

Seoul Olympic Park, Songpa-Gu, South Korea
Built in partnership with KACI International

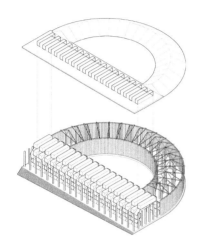

This unusual project with an area of 3455 square meters involved the combination of two of Shigeru Ban's favorite construction elements—structural paper tubes and used shipping containers—both of which represent a significant contribution to the reduction of the overall ecological impact of such a structure. Ban had already designed a temporary art exhibition facility with these elements (Nomadic Museum, Pier 54, New York, New York, USA, 2004–05; see page 62). Composed of a colonnaded, rectangular container structure ten meters high and a semicircular "Paper Gallery" enclosing an arc-shaped inner courtyard, Papertainer was a temporary exhibition pavilion for the celebration of the 30th anniversary of the Korean publisher Design House. The forested 14214-square-meter site was located in the Olympic Park of Seoul. The first "container wall" was intended for exhibition booths, while the second housed office and storage areas. The alternated placement of the containers, with regular voids, animated the main façade, while the paper tube colonnade in front of the structure gave it a gravitas that it might have lacked given the use of such industrial materials. The semicircular Paper Gallery was made of two walls composed of 75-centimeter-diameter paper-tube poles, with a roof truss made of 30-centimeter paper tubes.

Above:
A drawing shows the building with its roof and lower structure separated.

Opposite page:
As in the Nomadic Museum, containers and paper tubes form the structure.

Right:
An aerial view reveals the full scope of the semi-circular plan of the building.

2007 ▸ Takatori Church

Nagata, Kobe, Japan

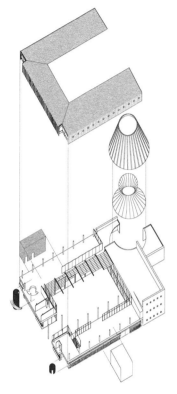

The new Takatori Church replaces the temporary Paper Church (1995; see page 38) built after the 1995 earthquake and recently reassembled in Taiwan. Shigeru Ban explains: "Interior and exterior can be connected by opening the sliding shutters that separate the courtyard from the low buildings around it. The chapel takes the form of a truncated cone, emerging from a corner and rising above the low-rise buildings." Although this new structure is more substantial than the original Paper Church, it has a lightness about it that signifies a continuity with the earlier architecture. Window shutters and projecting rooftop screens mark the architectural forms of what appears almost to be more a community center than a church in the more traditional sense. The limited means of the congregation obviously had an impact on the design, but this is precisely the kind of challenge that Shigeru Ban enjoys.

Above:
The inner design of the building seen in an exploded axonometric drawing.

Opposite page:
The interior of the chapel is flooded with natural light.

Right:
The inner courtyard at nightfall.

2006 ▸ Maison E

Iwaki, Fukushima, Japan

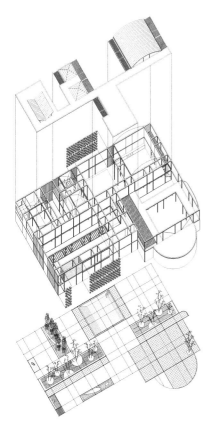

Although primarily a residence, the 1201-square-meter Maison E is also intended as a space for large receptions, which in part explains its floor area, quite ample by Japanese standards. This is also the case of the site area, which measures 1894 square meters. As he did in the Shutter House for a Photographer (Minato, Tokyo, Japan, 2002–03; see page 56), Ban employs a "tartan grid" alternating squares and rectangles, balancing interior spaces and courtyards, and resolving the issues posed by the division of private and public space. The main exterior materials of this two-story, steel-frame house are earth-colored brick painted white, glass panel shutters, aluminum louvers, and granite. Interior materials are plasterboard, limestone, wood flooring, and brick. A wooden vaulted ceiling is used in the main reception hall. As Ban says: "The look of the wooden vaulted ceiling is composed of wooden arches similar to medieval brick vaults, but by using solid laminated wood to express its thickness and shadow."

Above:
An exploded axonometric drawing of the house.

Opposite page:
Inner courtyards allow the house to be open to the sky while maintaining privacy.

Right:
An overall view of the Maison E.

2007 ▸ Nicolas G. Hayek Center

Chuo-ku, Tokyo, Japan

The new headquarters for Swatch Group Japan is a 14-story building in the fashionable Ginza shopping area, which has been marked in recent years by new buildings created by a number of well-known architects. It has a total floor area of 5697 square meters with areas for the seven watch brands of the group. The steel and reinforced-concrete building was designed between February 2005 and October of the same year. Four-story-high glass shutters articulate the front and back façades, opening to create a public passageway. A vegetal wall is installed in the atrium, where large glass "show-room" elevators serve each of the seven brand spaces. With its operable openings and green wall, the Nicolas Hayek Center marks a departure from the more traditionally designed small towers that line Ginza. Its exterior-interior ambiguities also give it a Japanese feeling that is lacking in other buildings usually designed for fashion houses.

Above:
The façade of the center with the glass shutters closed in the upper stories and open at ground level to reveal the public passageway.

Opposite page:
The tall, thin building is seen here in its typical Ginza setting, with all the glass shutters open.

Right:
The workings of the design are completely revealed by this drawing.

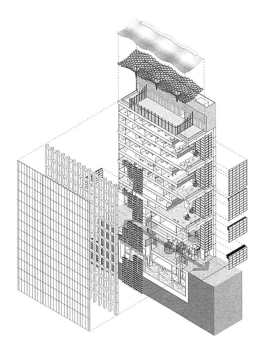

Left:
Four-story glass shutters make the heart of the building into a public passageway.

Below:
A vegetal wall marks the full height of the passage.

Above:
The hall on the 14th floor of the building with its curving lattice-work columns and ceiling.

Right:
The interior of the building houses seven different brand spaces.

2008 ‣ Hualin Temporary Elementary School

Chengdu, Sichuan, China

The so-called Great Sichuan Earthquake occurred on May 12, 2008, in the Sichuan province of China and killed at least 68 000 people, and possibly as many as 400 000. Students from banlab, the research center of Shigeru Ban, and the Hironori Matsubara Lab at Keio University used cardboard tubes to build temporary school buildings near Chengdu, with the collaboration of the Jiaotong University in that city. Three buildings, each with a 6 x 30-meter footprint, were created, each divided in three for a total of nine classrooms. The framework was made of paper tubes. Plywood with polycarbonate as insulation was employed for the roof. Students from Japan and China worked on the project over a 40-day period beginning in August 2008. This is the most recent instance of Shigeru Ban's assistance to areas where natural disasters have occurred.

Above:
Construction images show the very simple structure.

Opposite page:
Bright high spaces allow children to learn in pleasant circumstances despite the problems caused by the earthquake.

Right:
An overall view of the buildings of the school.

2010 ▸ Haesley Nine Bridges Golf Clubhouse

Yeoju, Gyeonggi, South Korea
Built in partnership with KACI International

The Nine Bridges Country Club Clubhouse, built in partnership with Kyeong-Sik Yoon (KACI International Inc.), is a 16 000-square-meter facility that serves a golf course. It has an underground level and three floors above grade. There is a main building, VIP lobby building, and a structure with private suites. The atrium and the upper portion of the main building include timber columns and a glass curtain wall, while the base is made of stone (random rubble masonry typical of Korea). The timber area includes the reception zone, a member's lounge, and a party room. The stone podium houses locker rooms, bathrooms, and service areas. The roof over the main building measures 36 x 72 meters. The unusual treelike timber columns in the atrium reach to a height of three stories. The partial-timber structure was used to conform to Korean regulations that do not allow timber buildings to exceed 6000 square meters in size. The first floor of the atrium has 4.5-meter-wide glass shutters that open fully.

Opposite page:
The generous and light interior space of the atrium.

Right:
Timber columns and roof are juxtaposed with a glass curtain wall.

Above:
Timber is used only in part of the structure because of local regulations.

Left and right:
A wooden lattice marks these interior spaces.

Opposite page:
Exterior views of the complex show its unusual variety of architectural features.

2007–10 ▸ Centre Pompidou-Metz

Metz, France

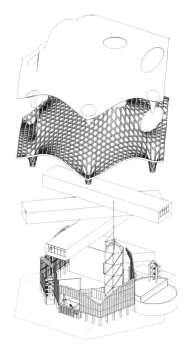

Shigeru Ban Architects (Tokyo) in association with Jean de Gastines (Paris) and Gumuchdjian Architects (London) won the design competition to build a new Centre Pompidou in the city of Metz on November 26, 2003. In this instance, Ban's surprising woven timber roof, based on a hexagonal pattern, was the most visible innovation, but his proposal to suspend three 90 x 15-meter gallery "tubes" above the required Grand Nef (nave) and Forum spaces was also unexpected and inventive. Working at the time of the competition on the Japan Pavilion (Expo 2000, Hanover, Germany, 1999–2000; see page 46), Shigeru Ban purchased a Chinese hat in a crafts shop in Paris in 1998. "I was astonished at how architectonic it was," says Shigeru Ban. "The structure is made of bamboo, and there is a layer of oil-paper for waterproofing. There is also a layer of dry leaves for insulation. It is just like architecture for a building. Since I bought this hat, I wanted to design a roof in a similar manner." Ban was anxious to participate in the original competition because of the involvement of the Centre Pompidou, whose architecture he had admired as being audacious for its time. Aside from its spectacular interior spaces, the Centre Pompidou-Metz is intended to open broadly onto its surrounding piazza, echoing the architect's frequent interest in the ambiguity of interior and exterior.

Above:
The stacked exhibition "tubes" can be seen in this drawing under the undulating roof.

Opposite page:
The roof rises up to greet visitors at the main entrance.

Right:
The structure stands out against the background of the old city, or stands alone, an unusual presence by any standard.

Above:
Visitors can view the underside of the roof and the upper surface of an exhibition gallery.

Left:
Spectacular interior spaces seen from the ground level.

Opposite page, above:
A section drawing reveals the stacked design.

Opposite page, below:
The entrance area can be opened entirely with operable glass shutters.

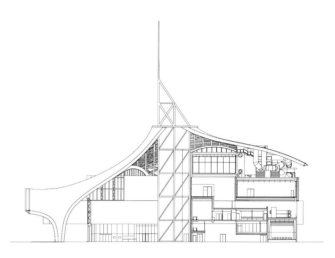

Above:
As visitors approach the large windows of the galleries, they have broad, framed views of the city.

Left:
Each gallery offers a generous view of the city—in this case of the cathedral, which unexpectedly appears to be more present as visitors see the window from a greater distance.

Opposite page, left:
Successive plans show the position of the layered galleries.

Opposite page, right:
Construction photos reveal the overall design of the complex roof.

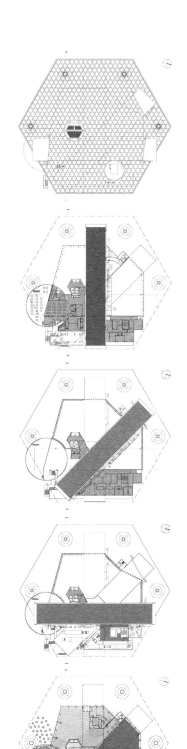

2010 ▸ Metal Shutter House

New York, New York, USA

Opposite page:
The façade of the building seen with the shutters partially open.

Below:
The building seen with its shutters in the closed and open positions.

Below right:
The interiors are spacious and airy, seen here with the shutters open.

The first condominium residence designed by Shigeru Ban in the United States, this 11-story building features duplex "houses" that can be opened fully to the exterior. Their double-height living rooms create an unusual amount of interior space. These are definitely luxury apartments. One of the apartments (Unit 6) has a floor area of 431 square meters, a full-floor duplex with four bedrooms, five bathrooms, a library and dining room, as well as five private outdoor areas. Located next to Frank O. Gehry's IAC Building and across the street from Jean Nouvel's latest condominium tower, the Metal Shutter Houses are part of one of the most talked-about new architectural areas in New York City. Although the building does not allow views toward the nearby Hudson River, the upper floors do look across a typical lower Manhattan roofscape with taller buildings in the distance. A well-known art gallery occupies the lower level spaces. Shigeru Ban collaborated with the New York architect Dean Maltz for this project, and also with the art dealer Klemens Gasser. This project marks the first permanent presence of Shigeru Ban in Manhattan.

2010 ▸ Villa Vista

Weligama, Sri Lanka

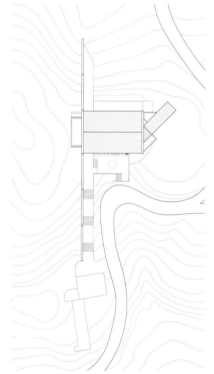

This house was designed for the owner of a tire company subsequent to Shigeru Ban's work on post-tsunami reconstruction in Sri Lanka. It is set on a hilltop site facing the ocean. The architect explains that there are three different framed views at the origin of the design: "The first is the view of the ocean seen from the jungle in the valley, framed perpendicularly by the external corridor from the existing house to this house and the roof. The next is the horizontal scenery of the ocean from the hilltop framed by the large roof supported by poles of 22-meter span and the floor. The last is the view of the cliff which glows red during sunset; this is viewed through a square frame composed of four meters of solid wood in the main bedroom." The roof is covered in light cement boards and woven coconut leaves that permit it to "blend into the local ambiance." Shigeru Ban created a woven "wickerwork" pattern for the ceiling of the residence with bands of teak 80 millimeters wide and 3 millimeters thick. Here, as always, the architect shows an ability to renew his style and structural approaches according to the task at hand.

Above:
A site plan with topographical curves showing the steep location.

Opposite page:
The house seen from sea level in its jungle setting.

Right:
The residence is imposing, mixing concrete and wood in an unusual way.

Above:
A generous view of the sea marks this image, with the woven teak ceiling also in evidence.

Right:
The architect willfully juxtaposes large opaque surfaces with openings that allow in light and air.

Opposite page, top:
An open stairway without rails leads to a deck that is at once inside and outside the house.

Opposite page, bottom:
A long dining table and a seating arrangement on the upper deck constitute the only furniture in this space.

2011 ▸ Paper Concert Hall

L'Aquila, Italy

On April 6, 2009, an earthquake measuring 6.3 on the Richter scale devastated the town of L'Aquila that is located 100 kilometers northeast of Rome. The building of the Conservatory of Music was amongst the structures destroyed by the earthquake, as was a renovated church that had served as a concert hall. Tubes made of recycled paper were employed as was the long-span steel-frame roof of an unused tram station. The project was announced as part of Japan's relief assistance on the occasion of the G8 Summit hosted by Berlusconi in L'Aquila in July 2009. Built with subscriptions from all over the world, the 3000-square-meter structure includes a temporary concert hall but also classrooms for the conservatory. Shigeru Ban writes: "It is planned that this temporary concert hall will be used for lectures and symposiums of the local university and also for other public events. And we hope this hall will be able to gather many musicians from around the world, help ease the hearts of victims, re-attract tourists, and moreover, that it will symbolize the revival of L'Aquila to people all over the world."

Above:
An axonometric drawing shows the colonnade and inner concert space.

Opposite page:
A view of the full structure above and of the red inner circle below.

Right:
The facility in use with its paper tube walls lining the space.

From top to bottom:
Shigeru Ban with his staff in Tokyo, Paris, and New York, 2012.

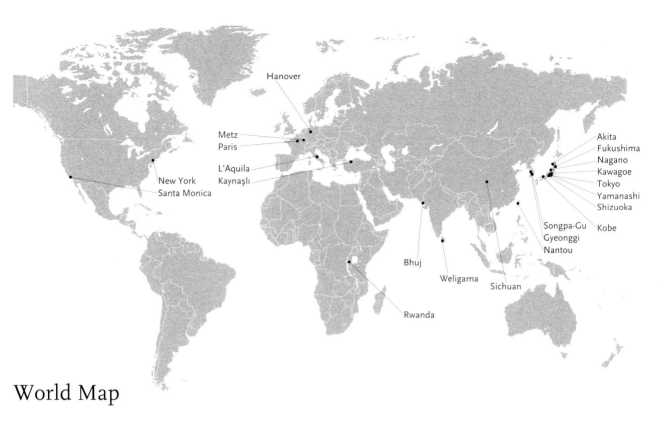

World Map

Life and Work

Bibliography

1998	*Paper Tube Architecture from Rwanda to Kobe*, Chikuma shobo Publishing Co., Ltd., Japan
	JA 30, Shigeru Ban, The Japan Architect, Japan
1999	*Shigeru Ban, Projects in Process*, TOTO Shuppan, Japan
2001	*Shigeru Ban*, Princeton Architectural Press, USA
2003	*Shigeru Ban*, Phaidon Press, New York/London
2008	*Shigeru Ban*, Edilstampa, Italy
2009	*Shigeru Ban: Paper in Architecture*, Rizzoli, New York
2010	*Voluntary Architects' Network*, INAX publication, Japan
	Shigeru Ban, Complete Works 1985-2010, Taschen, Germany
2011	*Shigeru Ban*, Hachette Fascicoli, Italy

Credits

The Author

Philip Jodidio studied art history and economics at Harvard, and edited *Connaissance des Arts* for over 20 years. His books include TASCHEN's *Architecture Now!* series, and monographs on Tadao Ando, Norman Foster, Richard Meier, Jean Nouvel, and Zaha Hadid. He is internationally renowned as one of the most popular writers on the subject of architecture.